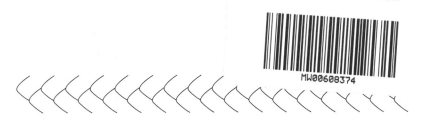
Love to Quilt...

Historical Penny Squares

Embroidery Patterns

Willa Baranowski

American Quilter's Society

P. O. Box 3290 • Paducah, KY 42002-3290

Located in Paducah, Kentucky, the American Quilter's Society (AQS), is dedicated to promoting the accomplishments of today's quilters. Through its publications and events, AQS strives to honor today's quiltmakers and their work – and inspire future creativity and innovation in quiltmaking.

Baranowski, Willa.
    Penny squares / by Willa Baranowski.
        p.   cm. -- (Love to quilt)
    Includes bibliographical references.
    ISBN 0-89145-879-4
    1. Patchwork--Patterns. 2. Quilting--Patterns. 3. Embroidery.
I. Title. II. Series.
TT835.B37 1996
    746.46'041--dc20   96-15932
                                            CIP

Additional copies of this book may be ordered from: American Quilter's Society,
P.O. Box 3290, Paducah, KY 42002-3290 @ $14.95. Add $2.00 for postage & handling.

DEDICATION
to the Southtowns Piecemakers Quilt Guild,
East Aurora, New York
My friends, neighbors, and supporters

ACKNOWLEDGEMENTS

Special thanks to Phyllis M. Rudz, who took my research, dream, and most of all, my many thoughts and tied them together so that this part of quilt history can be shared.

Thanks to Janet Myers and Bonnie Browning who encouraged me to print the information I've collected on Penny Squares.

Nancilu R. Burdick deserves special recognition for keeping me focused in completing this project.

And last, but certainly not least, thank you to my husband, John, for letting me be me.

Preface

In response to the many queries I have received at local and national quilt shows regarding Penny Squares or Redwork, I decided it is the right time to share what I have learned about the history of these ordinary muslin squares. As far as I know, there are no books regarding this subject and I believe this important part of quilt history should not be lost, and more importantly should be shared.

I have spent six years focusing on this subject, including lecturing, researching, teaching, and sharing patterns.

In this day of the information highway, it is important to remember the past. Through this book, I want to share the memories and thoughts people have shared with me when they remember the Penny Square.

This quilt art can play an important role in today's busy world, people need and want to create, but time is at a premium. Needlework should be relaxing and the simplicity of Penny Squares can be the answer to creating something special in a short span of time. Penny Squares are small, portable, simple to do, and addicting. Before you know it, you too can have enough squares to make a quilt or a wallhanging.

Through this book, I want to share the history of the circa 1915 Penny Square quilts (or Redwork). The book should appeal to quilt historians, creative, busy people, and most of all to pattern collectors.

The title *Penny Squares* tells of a time when life was simple and families shared activities. With this book, people will be able to create their own bit of history with the simple art of a Penny Square. It's a great way to share time and memories with young people and share your own thoughts for future generations.

Willa Baranowski

Contents

Introduction

September 1989 was a special time in my life. At our usual guild night, we had our show and tell segment of the meeting. From a shopping bag, one of our guild members removed a white and red cloth. Little did I know it would be the beginning of my addiction to Redwork, also known as the Penny Square.

Many of the guild members remembered seeing quilts like the one displayed and soon everyone was finding these small treasures. Some of the squares were already put together in quilts, but many of them were just stored and forgotten in attics, just waiting to be discovered...by me!

I began searching flea markets, garage sales, quilt shows, antique shops – the color red meant *stop* in more ways than one! However the more I looked, the more I realized that most of the history of these muslin squares came, not from books, but from word of mouth and the squares themselves. Dated and family quilts are great sources of information and if you're lucky, you'll meet a family member who remembers the muslin squares and the story of its background.

Penny Squares began to appear in 1880, and were popular throughout the early twentieth century. I concentrated my research on the pre-1915 Penny Square quilts and squares since they are very eclectic. Flowers, animals, baskets, famous people, and nursery rhymes were all used in the same quilt. Sets of patterns were not easily available until the 1920's.

In *Penny Squares* I hope to share my enthusiasm in this simple quilt art, sharing the thoughts of many people who made the squares when they were young, and help you create your own quilt of *penny thoughts*. It's a great way to share memories, history, and thoughts with your children or grandchildren. But most important, it's a way to leave a legacy of what life was like at the turn of a century...the twentieth or the twenty-first!

History

Life was still difficult in the late nineteenth century, despite rapid industrial development. Women were delegated to child care and homemaking chores. Days were filled with set routines for people living in the late 1800's and early 1900's. Every day of the week had a purpose: Mondays – wash; Tuesdays – iron; and of course shopping was done on Saturdays (Fig. 1). Children would accompany parents on Saturday shopping excursions. Children were taught needlework skills both at home and at school. It wasn't uncommon to see both girls and boys knitting, doing embroidery, and quilting.

Imagine a store lined with wooden shelves filled with anything and everything you might possibly want or need. That is the picture of the old general store, not unlike the mega-stores of today. In that general store, for the cost of one penny, a small muslin square could be purchased and a pattern could be printed on the square…that's how the term Penny Square was coined. Penny Squares were popular from the 1860's through the Depression years. They were also called Redwork since the squares were mostly embroidered with the popular Turkey red thread. It was a great learning tool for children and if you're fortunate to find a completed Penny Square quilt, you can see the progression of embroidery, from the simple tangled square to the final fine embroidered work.

Figure 1.

A pattern would be chosen from the shopkeeper's catalog book. Usually the shopkeeper would go into the back room where a selection of perforated paper patterns were kept. Perforated patterns were obtained from the Missouri-based Ladies' Art Company, established in 1898, with the publication of inexpensive pattern books or the Harper's Bazaar Sewing Catalog.

As each day had its specific purpose so did these perforated patterns. The smooth side was used in conjunction with a stamping wax. A cloth was dipped in gasoline and rubbed over colored wax blocks. This cloth was then rubbed over the smooth side of the perforated pattern and would leave a dotted design on the muslin square. If the rough side of the perforated pattern was placed on the muslin square a stamping

powder was used, usually blue or yellow. Stamping powder sold for fifteen cents a box. In some cases cinnamon was used to complete the design. If you see the same pattern in a reversed situation or if the letters are mirrored, chances are both the smooth and rough sides of the pattern were used (Fig. 2).

Prestamped muslin squares were also available, ranging in size from six inches to nine inches. Patterns could be simple or intricate, depending on how much money you had to spend.

Creating your own pattern was just as easy as tracing a picture from a magazine. With a sharp needle, a stamping pad filled with powder, or a soft pencil or crayon and iron, a person could make his own original design. Beginning around 1912, patterns could be purchased on preprinted fabric in groups of four from the Vogue Pattern Company and other companies. They were often arranged according to subject, such as animals or nursery rhymes.

DOG   DOG

Figure 2.

Types of Patterns

Penny Squares are often called "the forgotten quilt" of the 1900 era. Finding a collection of completed Penny Squares is like stepping back in time and reflecting on the simplicity of life at that time. Squares depicted the interests of the day and the pre-1915 Penny Square quilts were very eclectic. Flowers, animals, baskets, famous people, and nursery rhyme characters were all used in the same quilt. Perhaps buying the squares one at a time accounted for this varied style. In the 1920's quilt designers for catalogs and syndicated newspapers began to categorize their work. Therefore sets of flowers and Sunbonnet Sue series became popular, and a more organized look in Penny Square quilts began in the 1920 era.

Printed patterns were found, most notable in *Godey's Book* and magazine. Mail order was popular especially to rural people. The 1872 Montgomery Ward and 1891 Sears catalogs featured dry goods, fabrics, and batting. Specialty mail-order companies, such as H.M. Brockstedt, St. Louis, Missouri, produced simple patterns packaged in numbered gray waxed envelopes. Each pattern included templates and directions, and often a colored rendition of the quilt pattern painted on heavy cardboard, done by children earning extra money after school. If you're fortunate to find these painted pattern renditions, you have a treasure! The Brockstedt Company, started in 1875, was family owned and operated, and although the original owner died in the 1920's, the family continued the business until the 1940's.

Social messages of the day were seen on Penny Square quilts (Fig.3). Squares to commemorate certain events can also be found in quilts of that time. In 1901 a Pan American Exposition was celebrated in Buffalo, New York. A collection of squares was designed and sold to Expo visitors. These squares depicted various buildings specifically built for the expo, The Temple of Music (Fig. 4, page 10); midway attractions such as the Upside Down house (Fig. 5, page 11), and famous people who attended the expo, including President William McKinley, who sadly was assassinated at this event in 1901.

Flowers were also a popular pattern during this age. Each flower had a specific meaning and Victorian ladies consulted books on flower language, often sending secret messages through their needlework.

A Penny for your thoughts

A Temperance Drink

Figure 3.

Figure 4.

Temple of Music
Where President McKinley was shot

Roses are often found in Penny Square quilts. Legends abound regarding white and red roses. One of my favorites concerns the white rose, which is a symbol of charm, innocence, and silence or secrecy (Fig. 6, page 11). In ancient times a white rose was attached to the ceilings of council chambers to indicate secrecy. *Subrosa* today means, literally, "under the rose" – in legal terms, "in secret." Many of our court buildings today have a rosette in their ceiling decor.

Red roses are a sign of love and desire. Greek mythology claims that Aphrodite created a red rose from a white one when she pricked herself on a thorn and her blood changed the rose red.

Penny Squares were used as a learning tool to teach children embroidery as well as keep their hands busy. Many people remember doing them while convalescing during an illness. To make them appealing to children, the subject matter reflected what was important to them at that time. More ambitious and creative children drew their own pictures on muslin or traced them from books (Fig. 7, Log Cabin, page 12).

Among the most popular books were the Kate Greenaway series. Kate Greenaway was born in London, England, in 1846. She inherited her artistic talent from her father who was an engraver. At the age of 12, she had already won prizes from the National Gallery and British Museum of London, and began to design greeting cards depicting children wearing clothing from the 1812 era. With success came the imitators and Greenaway's drawings became fashion statements. Children's designs seen on many Penny Square quilts were taken from her book of verses *Under the Window*, published circa 1888 (Fig. 8, Girl with Hoop, page 12).

A Penny for your thoughts

House Upside Down

Figure 5.

A Penny for your thoughts

Figure 6.

11

Figure 7.

Figure 8.

Ruby Short McKim was a popular designer of this era. She is credited with being one of the most innovative and important quilt designers of the twentieth century. Most of her patterns were offered through syndicated newspapers. Her early quilt embroidery patterns reflected the very angular art deco style of that 1915 time frame. The Quaddy Quiltie was designed in collaboration with Thornton Burgess, the children's nature writer. He was the Ranger Rick of the early 1900's. The Quaddy Quiltie depicted his little woodland animals, with such names as Spotty the Turtle and Prickly Porky. These little characters appeared in many stories.

©Janet Myers 1994

Figure 9.

Using this same art deco design, Ruby McKim went on to design the Roly Poly Circus, Nursery Rhymes, Flower Garden, Audubon Birds, Colonial History, Bible History, and many others during the twenties. Her art style changed during the 1930's to a more realistic style. This is reflected in her nursery rhyme patterns. She designed a series of 24 nursery rhymes in 1916, then designed the Nursery Land Quilt in 1934. Both of these patterns contained exactly the same verses, but the art style was completely different with one having curved and the other straight lines.

Quilters today continue to imitate Ruby McKim's style. Janet Myers created her original version of Wee Willie Winkie using McKim's straight line style (Fig. 9).

Redwork

At the turn of the century, immigrants from Europe, especially Germany and the Alsace Lorraine area, brought with them many lovely linen pieces done in Turkey red, a thread commonly used in Europe. The logo depicted a turkey with the word red written across it (Fig. 10).

Many of these European pieces can be found today in their original form, with embroidered German phrases (Fig. 11). They are usually larger than the normal Penny Square and embroidered on linen or canvas fabric. These large pieces served useful purposes; splashes, (cloths hung behind dry sinks protecting the walls), and shams, protecting bedding during the day.

Turkey red not only denoted a color but a dye process which originated in Turkey centuries before.

A Penny for your thoughts

RED

Figure 10.

A Penny for your thoughts

Guten

Morgan

Guten

Nacht

Figure 11.

In the mid 1800's the dye process was introduced to Europe. The secret ingredient was the madder root, as well as cattle or sheep dung, rancid olive oil, sesame seed oil, alum, and even at times, blood. The dye process was lengthy with many details and took many months to complete. This intricate process paid off since Turkey red dye was virtually colorfast, in fact the color outlasted the life span of the material. This dye process was so complex, it was never carried out for commercial use in the United States.

Traditionally Penny Squares were embroidered in red. The thread was imported from

Europe as were most threads at that time. It came on a small wooden spool and can be compared to two strands of our present day embroidery floss.

Colored silk threads were used for fancy embroidery, but were quite expensive. Therefore the Turkey red was perfect for use in the simple Penny Square art. It was inexpensive, readily available, and most important, it did not run. The work was also called Redwork.

After 1920, the United States began manufacturing its own threads and more colors were available at better prices. Turkey red thread was no longer imported and an array of colors began appearing on embroidered quilts after 1920.

Stitching the Penny Square is very simple. The basic outline embroidery stitch is the popular choice. This stitch is also known as the Kensington stitch, named after an English needlework school. Since this stitch is quick and easy, children adapted to it readily. Chain, stem, fly, and feather stitches were also used in squares (Fig. 12).

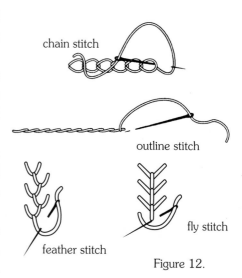

Figure 12.

Victorian women liked to embroider and embellish all manner of lines to decorate their homes and most importantly to show off their needlework skills. The crazy quilts of the late 1800's are a good study of the many embroidery designs and stitches. Many patterns used in crazy quilts found their ways into the simple Penny Squares. The peacock feather was a popular item to stitch in both types of work (Fig. 13).

Many lost thoughts and memories were recalled by a certain pattern design on a Penny Square quilt. You can also create your own memories for your children, grandchildren, or yourself by creating your own quilt. It is simple – patterns are included, or you can be creative by producing your own patterns. Imagine the thoughts and memories your Penny Square quilt or wallhanging will trigger in the year 2080!

Figure 13.

How to Make a Penny Square Quilt

MATERIALS
> unbleached muslin – enough to complete entire project
> #304 DMC – Turkey red
> small embroidery hoop (optional)
> freezer paper
> #2 lead pencil

TRANSFER PATTERN TO MUSLIN
> Cut 9" muslin squares.
> Cut 9" freezer paper squares.
> Find and mark the center of the freezer paper with an X.
> Find and mark the center of your pattern with an X.
> Press freezer paper to the wrong side of muslin square.
> Place on light table or glass top table with a lamp beneath, matching the center of the muslin square and the center of the pattern.
> Trace with a sharp #2 pencil or very thin mechanical pencil.
> Remove freezer paper; freezer paper may be reused many times.

Hints
> Cut all squares for your project at once from the same muslin yardage. All muslin is not alike. Dye lots and brand names need to be considered.
> Fold your 9" freezer paper into quarters to find the center.
> Use your 6" bias square to find and mark the center of your patterns.
> Use a fluorescent bulb in your lamp when tracing. This avoids burnt fingers from the heat of a regular light bulb onto the glass.

BEGIN TO EMBROIDER
> Place muslin square into a hoop (optional).
> Use 2 strands of #304 DMC (Turkey red) thread.
> Cut thread 12" – 16" long.
> Use 1 strand for detail, such as facial features or lettering.
> Use outline stitch to embroider pattern (Fig. 15).
> Enhance with other stitches as desired.

Figure 15.

Hints
> When using the outline stitch, keep your thread to the top or the bottom of your needle as you stitch. If you flip the thread back and forth, you will have an uneven, bumpy line.
> When going around an outside curve, keep your thread to the top of your needle (Fig. 16).

outside curve   inside curve

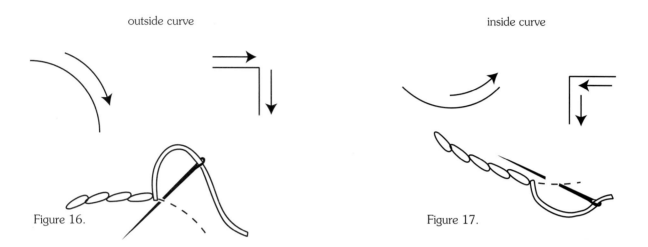

Figure 16.   Figure 17.

When doing an inside curve; keep thread to the bottom of your needle (Fig. 17).

When all blocks for a project are complete, press with a damp cloth on the wrong side. Square up the blocks to an 8" or 8½" block. This will depend on the amount of embroidery on your blocks. Sometimes if the block is heavily embroidered, the fabric shrinks up a bit.

Wait until all blocks are complete to square up to the desired size.

JOINING BLOCKS

Traditionally Penny Square blocks were joined block to block with no sashing. They were then feather-stitched over the seamline, tied with no batting, and used as summer coverlets.

I would like to present a few options that will update the Penny Square look a bit:

You may join your squares in groups of 4 or 9 to make a wallhanging (Figs. 19 and 20).

A grouping of 12 blocks creates a baby blanket size (Fig. 21).

Twenty-four or more will be a perfect throw, twin size, or larger.

Join your blocks to create the desired size.

Featherstitch over the seam lines.

Use 2 strands of Turkey red #304 DMC embroidery floss.

Hint

Featherstitching is usually worked along an imaginary center line. Put your needle in directly across from the last stitch and out diagonally down, on the same side of the imaginary center (seamline). Then repeat on the opposite side. Your stitch will swing from side to side. It takes a little practice to get into the groove!

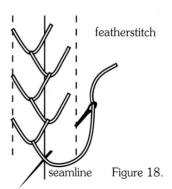

featherstitch

seamline   Figure 18.

17

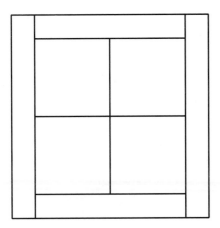

Four-Patch Wallhanging,
22" x 22"

Figure 19.

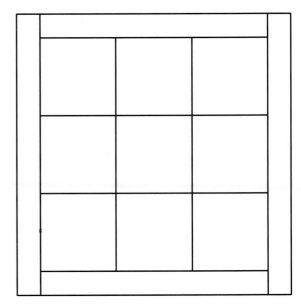

Nine-Patch Wallhanging,
30" x 30"

Figure 20.

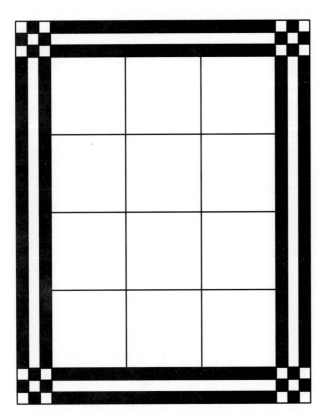

Baby or Crib size, 12 blocks,
30" x 38"

Figure 21.

BORDERS

Add a 3" red border all around.

Quilt as desired.

CHART FOR PENNY SQUARE QUILTS WITH FEATHERSTITCHING

No. of Blocks	Finished size	Borders	Yd. of Muslin	Yd. of Red
4	22" x 22"	2 – 3½" x 16½" 2 – 3½" x 22½"	¼ yd.	½ yd.
9	30" x 30"	2 – 3½" x 24½" 2 – 3½" x 30½"	½ yd.	¾ yd.
12	30" x 38"	2 – 3½" x 30½" 2 – 3½" x 38½"	1 yd.	1½ yd.
24	44" x 60"	2 – 6½" x 32½" 2 – 6½" x 60½"	1½ yd.	1¾ yd.

All border measurements include ¼ inch seam allowance.

Remembrances

Stories about the Penny Squares have been passed from one person to another to keep the history of them alive. As quiltmakers of today design their own Penny Squares, one can only imagine the stories future generations will hear. The following Remembrances share special stories related to Penny Squares.

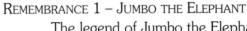

REMEMBRANCE 1 – JUMBO THE ELEPHANT

The legend of Jumbo the Elephant was a popular one depicted on many Penny Squares embroidered in the late 1800's. Jumbo, who resided in the London Zoo, was Queen Victoria's favorite animal. He was the largest African elephant in captivity and so gentle, children rode him at the zoo. In 1882, P.T. Barnum, of circus fame, purchased Jumbo for $30,000 and had him shipped to the United States. Queen Victoria was very upset, but unfortunately couldn't do anything to have Jumbo returned. Jumbo remained with the circus for three years as the main attraction. Tragedy occurred on September 15, 1885, in St. Thomas, Ontario, Canada. Jumbo, at the age of 24, was struck and killed by a runaway locomotive as the circus train was unloading. He is commemorated on many Penny Square quilts made during this time.

Figure 22.

REMEMBRANCE 2

At a quilt show, an elderly woman approached my booth and reminisced how she, her mother, and sister shopped for these Penny Squares. Both girls were given a penny to spend and had to do it wisely. She said that "if you chose a simple pattern it would be finished before the week was up, so more than likely, you'd like your penny to last an entire week and you would choose a more difficult pattern."

REMEMBRANCE 3

"I went to Souoder's General Store. They gave me a catalog and I picked out a picture, and they took it into another room and transferred that onto an unbleached muslin square. The embroidery hoop left a rust ring. There were pieces that you could buy in the store for five cents. Turkey red thread there came from Germany and then with World War I, the supply was cut off. Aunt Annie traced designs from magazines, this in a time when you could get nothing but red."

REMEMBRANCE 4

Joyce White from Williamsville, New York, related this Penny Square remembrance. At the turn of the century, scarlet fever was a common illness. If someone had scarlet fever, the entire household was quaran-

tined. Patients had to stay in their rooms in one part of the house, while the rest of the family stayed in another part. At Joyce's house, her grandmother was the only one allowed in the "sick bay area" since she had already had scarlet fever. A doctor visiting his patients would wash his hands and inhale a disinfectant before and after looking in on his patients. Meals were left in a certain area, and the patients would come and get them when everyone else was out of the way. While recovering, the children worked on Penny Squares to pass the time. However after recovery, these squares were burned for fear of carrying the scarlet fever germ.

Figure 23.

REMEMBRANCE 5 – SWAN

Swans were very popular in the late 1800's. Swan boats were introduced to the people on the public lakes in Boston, Massachusetts. The swan was used as a symbol of the Women's Educational and Industrial Union formed after the Civil War in Boston by Dr. Harriet Clisby. This organization was formed to help women survive on their own after the war, by learning various sewing skills and providing an outlet to sell them. This organization exists today, and a Boston store still sells women's handiwork.

REMEMBRANCE 6 – YOUNG LADY

This lovely young lady with the beautiful curls has appeared on many quilts, as early as 1875 (Fig. 24).

REMEMBRANCE 7

Children played and sorted Penny Squares until they were made into coverlets. Some of the squares remained playthings and remained in a box tucked in the attic for future children to enjoy and hopefully put together in a coverlet as intended. This makes it a two or three generation project.

Figure 24.

A Penny for your thoughts

Tufted Titmouse

Figure 25.

REMEMBRANCE 8

Sharon Witt of Orchard Park, has a coverlet that is much loved and worn. During the 1920's her grandmother's sister suffered from epilepsy. Since little was known of the illness at that time, she was kept hidden from the community. In order to keep her busy and provide pin money for her, she embroidered Penny Squares, and had them quilted by someone else. Her coverlet is treasured today and is used as a comfort blanket when someone is ill.

REMEMBRANCE 9 – BILLY'S QUILT

My mother-in-law passed away in 1967 when I was pregnant with my son. While going through her possessions beside her bed, I found a complete set of original newspaper patterns for a Nursery Rhyme quilt, published in 1934. Apparently she had started this project while she was pregnant with my husband (who was born in 1934), but had never completed it. In 1967, she apparently started working on it again to give to my son, her grandchild, Billy. There were ten partially completed blocks and squares, and I have since finished it.

A Penny for your thoughts

Astor Cup

Vigilant

Figure 26.

REMEMBRANCE 10 – VIGILANT

The Vigilant, owned by the John Astor family, was the sailing ship which won the America's Cup Race in 1893. The award was the Astor Cup, one that is still awarded for cup races.

Remembrance 11

During a quilt show in Lancaster, PA, a cat fancier from England visited my booth. She attends quilt shows primarily to find cat patterns, fabric, buttons, etc., appeasing her love of cats. (She has 24 of them!) Naturally she was drawn to the square depicting the cat whose paw is in the fishbowl. She recognized this pattern as one seen on hand-painted china during a visit to a British museum. This was a popular pattern done on blue and white china.

Figure 27.

Remembrance 12

Times were difficult and people were very thrifty. A quilt dated 1913 shows Penny Squares with imperfectly stamped designs. Rather than throw away the imperfect pattern, a local shopkeeper brought them home for his daughters to embroider and a quilt resulted from this penny pinching.

Remembrance 13 – Dolly Dingle

Dolly Dingle was a cartoon character created by Grace Drayton in 1914. Dolly was often shown with her dog, Comfy. Many squares depict Dolly and her dog doing everyday happenings. Now, Dolly plays an important role in counseling abused children. Social workers use Dolly and Comfy as role models showing how to get along and share a kind, caring existence. The roly poly children of the Campbell Soup ads bear a strong resemblance to Dolly, as they also were created by Grace Drayton.

Figure 28.

REMEMBRANCE 14 – LUCKY HORSESHOE

Horseshoes are a symbol of luck, but make sure you keep all the luck. Position your pattern with the open end up to keep your luck inside, otherwise it will fall out the bottom.

Good Luck!

Figure 29.

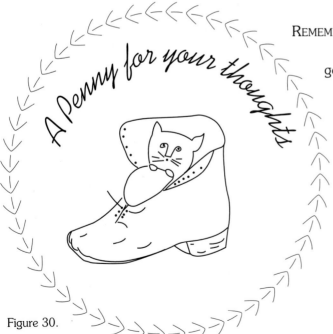

REMEMBRANCE 15 – KITTEN IN A SHOE

Kittens in a boot were believed to be a sign of good luck at the turn of the century. This little guy has made many showings on quilts of that era.

Figure 30.

REMEMBRANCE 16 – USS NEW YORK

The USS New York was a battleship commisioned in 1911, and was still in service during World War II in the 1940's. It was the first ship to be built using armoured steel on the decks.

U.S.S. New York

Figure 31.

REMEMBRANCE 17

Two sisters slept under a Penny Square quilt as they were growing up. Each night the younger sister would choose a picture block. The older sister would then make up a story to go with the block as a bedtime story.

REMEMBRANCE 18 – THE PENNY SQUARE

This is the ultimate in Penny Square designs. This design originated in Ruby McKim's Colonial History Quilt of 1926. It is a stamp of Great Britain which was printed on all goods coming into the new Americas before the American Revolution. It was the stamp that brought on the Stamp Act and fueled the fires of the American Revolution.

Figure 32.

Gallery

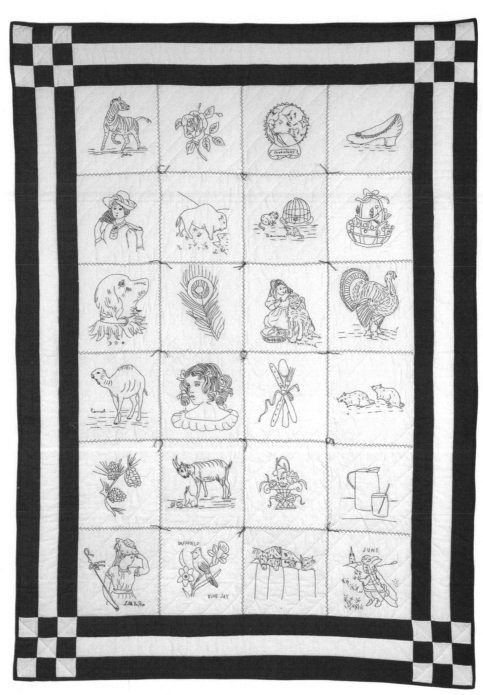

Plate 1.

Plate 2.

Plate 3.

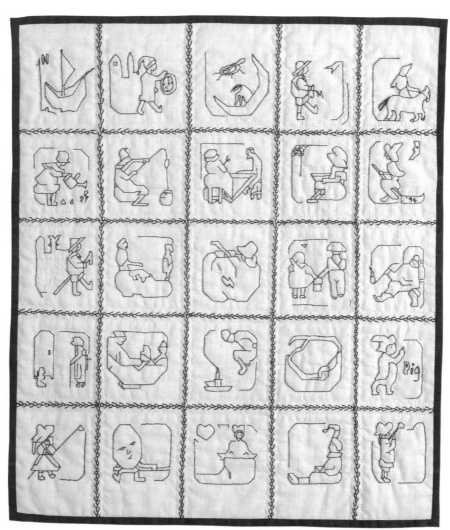

Plate 4.

Animal Patterns

JUMBO

Camel

Who'll get the worm?

Donkey

Zebra

Basket & Fruit Patterns

Blue Bird

Hummingbird

Flower Patterns

Your
Name,
Date,
Message

Victorian Patterns

 # Bibliography

Books

Atkins, Jacqueline M., and Phyllis A. Tepper. *New York Beauties*. Dutton Studio Books, 1992.

Brackman, Barbara. *Clues in the Calico*, EPM Publications, Inc., 1989.

Martin, Nancy. *Threads of Time*, Patchwork Place.

McMorris, Penny. *Crazy Quilt*, E.P. Dutton Inc., 1984.

Montano, Judith. *The Crazy Quilt Handbook*, C & T Publishing, 1988.

Plowden, Gene. *Those Amazing Ringlings and Their Circus*. Caxton Printers, Ltd. 1968.

Roan, Nancy Ann and Ellen J. Gehret. *Just a Quilt/ or Juscht en Deppich*, Goschenhoppen Historians Inc., Green Lake, PA 1993.

Articles

Benberry, Cuesta. "Quilt Patterns of the Late Victorian Era Part II and III," *Nimble Needles Treasures*, Spring 1973.

Munsey, Sandra G. and Nancy Roberts. "Redwork Quilts," *Traditional Quiltworks*, #32, 1994.

Stehlik, Jan. "Quilt Pattern and Contests of the Omaha World – Omaha Herald 1921–1941," *Uncoverings*, 1990 Volume II of the Research Papers of the American Quilt Study Group.

_____ "Town Pays Tribute to 'Peter Rabbit' Creator," *Nimble Needle Treasures*, 1974.

AQS BOOKS ON QUILTS

This is only a partial listing of the books on quilts that are available from the American Quilter's Soceity. AQS books are known the world over for their timely topics, clear writing, beautiful color photographs, and accurate illustrations and patterns. Most of the following books are available from your local bookseller, quilt shop, or public library. If you are unable to locate certain titles in your area, you may order by mail from the AMERICAN QUILTER'S SOCIETY, P.O. Box 3290, Paducah, KY 42002-3290. Customers with Visa or MasterCard may phone in orders from 7:00–4:00 CST, Monday–Friday, Toll Free 1-800-626-5420. Add $2.00 for postage for the first book ordered and $0.40 for each additional book. Include item number, title, and price when ordering. Allow 14 to 21 days for delivery.